POCKET **Jokes**

POCKET **Jokes**

collected by
**Phillip Adams
& Patrice Newell**

PENGUIN BOOKS

Penguin Books Australia Ltd
487 Maroondah Highway, PO Box 257
Ringwood, Victoria 3134, Australia
Penguin Books Ltd
Harmondsworth, Middlesex, England
Viking Penguin, A Division of Penguin Books USA Inc.
375 Hudson Street, New York, New York 10014, USA
Penguin Books Canada Limited
10 Alcorn Avenue, Toronto, Ontario, Canada M4V 3B2
Penguin Books (N.Z.) Ltd
182–190 Wairau Road, Auckland 10, New Zealand

First published by Penguin Books Australia Ltd 1996

2 4 6 8 10 9 7 5 3 1

This selection, introduction and other original material,
copyright © Phillip Adams and Patrice Newell, 1996

All rights reserved. Without limiting the rights under copyright
reserved above, no part of this publication may be reproduced,
stored in or introduced into a retrieval system, or transmitted, in
any form or by any means (electronic, mechanical, photocopying,
recording or otherwise), without the prior written permission of
both the copyright owner and the above publisher of this book.

This book contains a selection of jokes previously published in
The Penguin Book of Australian Jokes.

Typeset in Formata Regular and Agenda Light Condensed
by Post Typesetters
Printed and bound in Australia by Australian Print Group,
Maryborough

National Library of Australia
Cataloguing-in-Publication data

Pocket jokes.
ISBN 0 14 026207 5.
1. Wit and humour. I. Adams, Phillip, 1939– .
II. Newell, Patrice, 1956– .
808.882

ABOUT THE AUTHORS

Phillip Adams is a writer, film-maker and broadcaster who calculates that he has published 15 million words in his long career as a newspaper columnist. He was recently seen discussing the 'Big Questions' with Professor Paul Davies in the SBS TV series of the same name. Recent books include *The Penguin Book of Australian Jokes* and *The Penguin Book of Jokes from Cyberspace*, both compiled with Patrice Newell, a former television researcher, newsreader and presenter of public affairs programmes who, these days, raises beef on a remote cattle property.

EDITORS' NOTE

Most of these jokes have been reprinted in much the form we heard or received them in the hope of preserving something of their spirit, not to mention the hope of maintaining archaeological interest in the cultural bigotries of our time.

CONTENTS

Introduction 1

PART **One** Laughter in the House 7
  Politicians' Creed 8
  Politicians on Politicians 10
  Politicians at Home 17
  Politicians Away 35

PART **Two** The Laugh's on Others 45
  Bush & Country Folk 46
  Professional Carers 62
  Money-brokers & Money-spenders 71
  Creative Industry Types 80
  Religious Beings 87

PART **Three** Political(ly) Incorrect 93
  Racism 94
  Sexism 106

The Last Laugh 119

INTRODUCTION

The last time I actually bumped into Bob Hawke was at Mascot Airport, early on a Friday morning. I was nodding off in an Ansett lounge, waiting for a Hobart flight. Someone came in and sat opposite – I recognised him as Sir Tristan Antico. We exchanged slight smiles. He made a phone call, in fluent Italian.

I recall that I was squinting at my daily dose of *Doonesbury*, the great comic strip by Garry Trudeau, when a third person arrived in the lounge. I couldn't help but notice because he immediately started screaming obscenities at me.

I learnt that I combined putrefaction with illegitimacy and was a copulating pudendum. At the same time I managed to be a combination of penis and cranium. My accuser/abuser was standing over me, his threatening proximity emphasising the tirade which, remarkably, continued to escalate.

When I mildly suggested to the enraged wild-eyed interrupter of *Doonesbury* that he combine urination with departure, he managed to increase both volume and venom reaching his climax with the suggestion that I was engaging in a consenting adult relationship with Gough Whitlam which, in turn, had clouded my vision. And, indeed, if my head had been in the position suggested by the enraged Rumplestiltskin prancing before me, it would have been very hard to see anything. It would also have been impossible to breathe.

You've guessed. You know who was screaming at me. Yes, an undergraduate from the John Singleton School of Charm. A previous prime minister of Australia who, only yesterday, would ring me at home on Christmas Day. Then I was in the good books. Now I was cast into outer darkness.

Yet I am still considerably in his debt. For it was Bob who, in a more cordial encounter, when he was still ensconced at the Lodge, posed me the following riddle:

> There are two squashed corpses on the Hume Highway. One is a dead possum, the other a dead politician. What's the difference?
>
> There are skid marks before the possum.

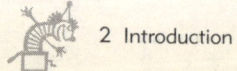

I would later learn that this joke had begun its life in the US. There the highway was Route 66 and the dead animal, a skunk.

Nonetheless the joke seemed to me, at the time, characteristically Australian. And on that basis I decided to contact the politicians across this wide brown land and ask for others.

My partner, Patrice Newell, sat down and wrote letters to every MP in state and federal parliament. Would they be kind enough to send us a favourite joke? Soon the replies came flooding in although, sad to say, most of the pollies confused jokes with anecdotes and sought to share with us some allegedly amusing electoral encounters.

Nonetheless, we found that many politicians had provided us with politically incorrect jokes. And so, along with contributions from other sources, *The Penguin Book of Australian Jokes* was born.

To our astonishment, and to Penguin's, the book became a bestseller. Not only of the year, but of the decade. But in that book the sources of the jokes were concealed. Readers had no way of knowing which joke was provided by a politician, which by a cardinal, or which by a rock star.

In this little book we've decided to come clean with some

of the jokes. More, perhaps, to come grubby. We will identify, 'out', a selection of those who provided the jokes because, very often, there's something of a joke in that.

Many of the jokes in this collection came from politicians. But we've also included jokes from famous and/or notorious people from other professions. For example, there's a collection of jokes from Rolf Harris.

I like Rolf very much. I first met him just after the release of 'Tie Me Kangaroo Down', when he was still working as a schoolteacher. I found the song amusing and wanted to buy it for a Melbourne bakery, Home Pride. Rolf sold me the rights and his sacred song, up there with 'Waltzing Matilda' as an unofficial national anthem, was crudely parodied. The new lyrics went: 'It's gotta be Home Pride bread, Fred' and the TV commercial by Alex 'Life. Be In It' Stitt depicted a bread-eating buffoon who happened to be a caricature of a mutual friend, Fred Schepisi.

Since then Rolf has become a megastar. So enormous is his cultural influence that he performed, for Australia, at the United Nations, and has been multiplied endlessly on a program of *The Goodies*. Perhaps you saw it – hundreds of identical Rolf Harrises filled the landscape, to the very horizon. Now we shall reveal that Rolf, this wholesome, thoroughly decent ambassador for this once great nation, tells appalling jokes. Tasteless, crude, vulgar, politically incorrect.

This will probably destroy his career. It will not be the first time an activity of Adams's has cruelled the pitch of an Australian entertainer. Older readers might recall a fine documentary of the early 1970s, comparable in anthropological excellence to anything of Margaret Mead's, concerning the life and times of Barry McKenzie, an interesting example of Australian fauna. My partners in the project, Bruce Beresford and Barry Humphries, decided that the big-chinned Crocker had been born to play his well-known namesake and so commissioned the hapless, hatless entertainer to don the McKenzie Akubra. Little did we – or Crocker – know that the film would have a shattering effect on the young man's career. Having dominated the Mother's Day market for years – a Crocker LP was almost as suitable a gift as an album by one of those Scottish tenors – Crocker saw his sales go down the gurgler. Outraged by images of their favourite performer dropping his daks on the BBC and pointing his percy at any amount of porcelain, the blue-rinse market deserted him in their droves, turning to Kamahl. And, yes, to Rolf Harris.

Sorry, Rolf. Bang goes the Mother's Day market. But the public has a right to know.

Where possible we will also show how jokes bounce around the planet, being told and retold, recast and relocated.

Let the jokes lie where they fall.

PART **One**

Laughter in the House

POLITICIANS' CREED

Once upon a time, a little non-conforming swallow decided not to fly south for the winter. He was unsure of the rationale behind the annual pilgrimage of his contemporaries and, being suspicious of unproved advice, decided to test the claim that it was necessary to avoid the life-threatening winter. So he wouldn't budge.

Gradually the winter started to close in. The swallow grew colder and colder. Finally he decided to head south after the others. But he'd left it too late. As he flew, the winter became more and more bitter. Ice formed on his wings. Eventually, he fell to earth in a frost-covered field. As he gasped his last breath, a cow wandered through the field and crapped on him. The warmth of the manure thawed his wings, warmed his body and revived him. He was so overjoyed by this turn of events that he raised his little head and whistled a happy little bird song. Just at that moment, a cat walking through the field heard the happy little chirping sound. It found the mound of dung, uncovered the little swallow and ate him.

There are three morals to this story:
1. Everyone who craps on you is not necessarily your enemy.
2. Everyone who extricates you from crap is not necessarily your friend.
3. If you are warm and comfortable in a pile of crap, keep your mouth shut.

FROM BOB BROWN. No, not that Bob Brown, the other one. From the Hon. Robert James Brown, BEc, DipEd, who went from a mining town into the Hawke ministry.

POLITICIANS ON POLITICIANS

A businessman, disappointed in his career, decided to volunteer for the first brain transplant. A brilliant surgeon offered him a choice of three samples from his brain bank: one from a leading brain surgeon at $1000, one from a leading research scientist at $1000 and one from a retired politician at $5000. He enquired why the last one was so much dearer. 'It's never been used,' said the brain surgeon.

FROM THE HON. Doug Everingham, a member of the Whitlam ministry.

Q. If an intelligent politician, an intelligent woman and the Easter Bunny got into a lift together and discovered a $10 note lying on the floor, who would pick it up?

A. The intelligent woman. The other two don't exist.

FROM THE HON. Michael Walter Field, BA, one of the ex-premiers of Tasmania who seemed to pass by the consciousness like the uprights in a post-and-rail fence.

Information was received that a professor at a local university had decided to use politicians in the laboratory to replace rats in experimentation. The professor gave three reasons:

'Firstly, in this modern day and age of improved hygienic conditions I have found that there are fewer rats in the community than politicians. Secondly, in my long experience with handling rats I've grown fond of them, whereas I do not have this difficulty with politicians. Finally, however, after years of working with rats I have been frequently frustrated because, frankly, there are some things rats will not do.'

FROM THE HON. Ted Pickering, BSc, FAIE, MAus/MM, MLC, ex-Minister for Police and Emergency Services in the Greiner government, driven into private life by the unstinting efforts of the NSW police force, particularly its then commissioner, Tony Lauer.

Three plastic surgeons

meet at a conference. The first, an American, talks about the latest triumph in Californian reconstruction. 'A guy was shot to pieces in a shoot-out. All we had left was his right ear. We took that ear, reconstituted the entire body and now he's back at work. As a matter of fact, he's replaced six men.'

The English plastic surgeon promptly tops the story. 'We had a nuclear accident at a power station, and all that was left was a single hair. We took that hair, reconstructed the entire human being and now he's back at work at the power station where he's replaced *twenty* men.'

The Australian plastic surgeon is unimpressed. 'I was walking down Collins Street a few weeks ago and smelt a fart. I trapped it in a bottle, got back to the hospital, managed to constitute it into an arsehole and then into an entire human body. That bloke's now the Prime Minister of Australia, and he's put a million people out of work.'

A medical doctor, an engineer and a politician were discussing their professions. Which profession was the oldest?

The medical officer reminded the others that the Book of Genesis clearly states that the first woman was created from the rib of a man. This was a medical function, so one must agree that his profession was the oldest.

Whereupon the engineer argued that earlier in the Book of Genesis there was reference to the fact that God created order and calm out of chaos and mayhem. 'That would take an engineer!'

'Oh no,' cried the politician. 'We go back further. Who do you think created the chaos?'

RECEIVED FROM Kenneth Alastair (Ken) Coghill, BVSc, past Speaker in the Victorian Legislative Assembly.

The political candidate knocked hopefully on the door of a prospective supporter in the electorate and introduced himself. Much to his surprise, the lady of the house remarked: 'I'm certainly not going to vote for you!'

'But,' said the candidate, 'you've never seen my opponent.'

'No,' said the lady, 'but I've had a damn good look at you.'

FROM THE LATE and greatly loved Fred Daly. The Hon. Frederick Michael Daly, AO, was one of parliament's most notable wags and his books, after retirement, included *The Politician Who Laughed*.

It happened in the early 1970s. There was this almighty flood. In one of the rescue helicopters – apart from the pilot – there was an odd group of three people. A young hippie, a simple country clergyman and a half-sozzled bloke in a crumpled suit. Suddenly the machine developed a serious fault. Ashen-faced, the pilot turned around and said: 'I'm terribly sorry, but you'll have to bail out because we're going to crash. The problem is that we've only got two parachutes.'

Before he finished speaking, the business-suited bloke spoke up: 'I'm a Rhodes scholar,' he said, 'and I'm in charge of all the workers in Australia. I have the brains, the drive and the connections to become the PM of this great country. I am clearly indispensable.' So saying, he grabbed the pack nearest to hand and jumped out.

'Son,' said the padre, 'I am an old man, I suffer from arthritis and am near the end. You have your life ahead of you – you take the other parachute.'

'What's with you, man?' asked the hippie, 'there's still two chutes. That self-important idiot jumped out with my back-pack.'

SUBMITTED BY the Hon. Joan Marjorie Coxsedge, MLC for Melbourne West and feisty member of Labor's left.

POLITICIANS AT HOME

Q. What's the difference between having your hand down the front of Bob Hawke's trousers and driving a Volvo?

A. You'll feel a bigger prick in a Volvo.

THIS JOKE ARRIVED on embossed letterhead from Government House in Canberra. While it bears an eerie similarity to recent revelations in Bill Hayden's autobiography, the erstwhile Governor-General denies all knowledge of the invidious comparison above.

To Sir John Falstaff, c/- Phillip Adams Esquire. Having exiled one Sir John, am not amused at arrival of another. You will find Melbourne massage parlours are no improvement on Boar's Head Tavern. We university wits will not pander to your ribaldry... Hal Whitlam.

A FAX TO Gough Whitlam, c/- Australian National University cloisters, requesting a contribution to our book elicited the foregoing reply. During Gough's time as prime minister, we'd corresponded as Hal Whitlam and Falstaff Adams.

Paul Keating was tripping along a country road when the car ran over a pig. He told the chauffeur to go to the nearby farm house and explain what had happened, apologise and offer to pay for the animal.

The driver was gone a long time and when he returned had lipstick all over his face, was smoking a cigar and clutching an empty champagne bottle.

'I had a marvellous time boss,' he said. 'The farmer gave me a cigar, his sons kept giving me champagne and his daughters made passionate love to me.'

'Good grief,' exclaimed Paul, 'what on earth did you say to them?'

'Just what you told me, boss,' said the chauffeur. 'I knocked on the door and said "G'day, I'm Paul Keating's chauffeur and I've just killed the pig."'

FROM THE HON. Francis Leslie (Frank) Madill, MB, BS, FRACGP, who is something of an over-achiever in Tasmania, in that his ministries since 1992 have included (count them) Police and Emergency Services, Consumer Affairs, and Multicultural and Ethnic Affairs. He's also been Minister Assisting the Premier.

'He's always been insufferable. In fact, he was so insufferable as a child that at the age of nine both parents ran away from home.'

①

'When he was born he was so unprepossessing that his parents hired a team of lawyers to try to find a loophole in his birth certificate.'

FROM THE HON. Gareth John Evans, BA, MA, LLB, QC, Foreign Minister in the Hawke and Keating governments, whose 'favourite jokes are one-liners which can be pinned more or less at random on one's political opponents.' He interchanges the above jokes for Joh Bjelke-Petersen or Malcolm Fraser. Like Bob Hawke, jokes have got Gareth Evans into considerable trouble from time to time.

Q. Why do people take an instant dislike to Bronwyn Bishop?

A. Because it saves time.

FROM GARETH AGAIN. Not so random this time.

I was driving through the Victorian countryside a couple of years ago. With the honesty of a Democrat I conceived [*sic*] my speedometer needle was perilously close to 120 kph. On the left-hand side of the road I noticed two typical eleven-year-old boys. At eleven years of age, boys seem to achieve their most unspeakable and insufferable and, yet, most lovable selves. They also seem to master the cheekiest of toothy grins. These two chaps were no exception. They were wearing red *Herald*-peaked caps and holding up a large home-made sign roughly printed in texta colour 'SLOW DOWN POLICE CHECK AHEAD'. Instinctively my foot came off the accelerator and I negotiated the next bend within the speed limit. As I passed the police trap, complete with radar and other paraphernalia, I remember giving a royal wave and the smuggest of smiles. I was having some thoughts of these altruistic lads when I passed the next bend. Here on the left-hand side of the road were two other eleven-year-olds with a roughly printed sign 'NOW WASN'T THAT WORTH THE BUCK'.

SUPPLIED BY the Hon. Donald Leslie Chipp, AO, who, having been minister to the Navy, Tourism, Trade, Customs, Social Security, Health, Repatriation and Compensation, left the Libs to lead the Australian Democrats from 1978 to 1986.

22 Laughter in the House

Nick Greiner was having great difficulty getting any good press coverage. So he called his press secretary and demanded that all the press be assembled under the Harbour Bridge for a major announcement at noon the next day.

The due time arrived and all the state's media were assembled. The Premier said: 'I'm sick and tired of all this bad coverage, so I'm going to do something that nobody here can complain about.' He then proceeded to walk on the water across Sydney Harbour.

The Premier awoke next morning to find that the *Sydney Morning Herald* proclaimed: 'GREINER CAN'T SWIM' while the *Telegraph* was emblazoned with the banner 'GOVERNMENT RORTS: GREINER DOESN'T PAY THE TOLL'.

FROM THE HON. James Alan (Jim) Longley, BEc, MEc, FCPA, whose ministries in NSW included Community Services, and Aboriginal Affairs.

Tim Fischer, Deputy Prime Minister.

A JOKE FROM the recently
elected Prime Minister, the
Hon. John Winston Howard.

Alexander Downer, Foreign Minister.

ANOTHER JOKE FROM the same source.

After the late Tim Jackson, a former leader of the Liberal Party, retired from Parliament, he became internationally known for producing some of the world's best daffodils. As such he was often asked if he could send daffodil bulbs around the world but, in most cases, they'd perish before they'd arrive.

As the years rolled on, Tim became more and more crippled with arthritis and needed to use his crutches to get around. This disability did not deter him from his enthusiasm for producing daffodils and one day he struck upon a perfect way to export the bulbs – he used a condom with a little water in it. The daffodil arrived at its destination hail and hearty. Having proof that the experiment worked he then collected all his orders, which amounted to 144.

On a Friday evening he walked with some difficulty into the local chemist shop, and asked the chemist for 144 condoms, not explaining the purpose to which he intended putting them. The chemist was somewhat taken aback but handed over the cache. Tim spent the weekend filling each condom with a daffodil and, as well, received a phone call from a customer ordering a further 144 bulbs.

Tim returned to the chemist on Monday morning and asked him for another 144 condoms, adding: 'And this time give me 144. You short-changed me by five on Friday night!'

NOT TO BE confused with the Hon. William Michael Hodgman, the 'Mouth from the South', this joke was submitted by the Hon. Peter Curtis Leigh Hodgman, Minister for Tourism, Sport and Recreation, Status of Women, Construction, Administrative Services, the Environment and Inland Fisheries in various Tasmanian governments – thus nudging Frank Madill from the Taswegian edition of the Guinness Book of Ministerial Records.

Sir Henry Winneke

had just been appointed Governor of Victoria. The Liberal Minister, Murray Burn, was promptly approached by the Master of the Masonic Lodge to arrange the attendance of the new Governor and his wife at a ladies' night. Murray, a Catholic, jumped at the opportunity, saying: 'I've always wanted to see what this riding the billy goat is all about.' The dinner duly took place with Sir Henry chatting racily throughout the evening to the Master's wife, whilst the Master himself was being attentive to Lady Winneke. With coffee, Lady Winneke had a liqueur, and when she put down the glass the Master turned to her and said: 'Will you have another Winneke, Lady Drambuie?' 'No thanks,' she replied, 'one Winneke a night is enough for me.'

FROM THE HON. Alan John Hunt, AM, a long-serving minister in Victorian Liberal governments.

A prostitute decides to undertake a new marketing technique by applying tattoos to her inner thighs. On one thigh is tattooed the face of Nick Greiner, on the other that of Wal Murray. Any client identifying one or the other receives a 50 per cent discount. If they could identify both, they got a freebie. A succession of customers identify either Nick or Wal. Then the lady happens to pick up an off-duty policeman who couldn't recognise either. 'Nup, I give up,' he says. 'But the one in the middle looks like Ted Pickering.'

FROM WENDY MACHIN, BA, MP, minister in the Fahey government. Ms Machin reports that everyone in cabinet enjoyed the joke, except for Ted.

During the Fraser years, when John Stone still led the Treasury, a small dispute between clerical officers and the government resulted in a one-man picket at the bottom of the Treasury steps. The lone picketer was having limited success convincing his fellow unionists to join the strike, but even Stone's arrival at work did not deter him. 'SCAB!' he called after Stone, who turned around to give the striker a lengthy lecture about the distortion of allocation of labour, the imbalanced power of unions and the benefits of government labour policy. Satisfied he had made his point, Stone continued up the stairs only to hear the cry 'SCAB!' again at his back. Patiently he returned to the picketer and again (with more emotion) gave the man a diatribe on the many benefits of Tory labour policy. This time the striker would surely understand. Stone returned to his climb up the stairs. 'SCAB!' the call came for the third time. Exasperated, Stone returned to the picket, saying with conviction: 'You have heard my views. I just don't know what to say to people like you,' and he turned on his heel to stomp up the stairs. The picketer paused before calling after Stone: 'INARTICULATE SCAB!'

FROM SENATOR THE HON. Nick Bolkus, LLB, Minister for Immigration and Ethnic Affairs in the Keating government.

SPACE RESERVED FOR A JOKE FROM THE RT HON. JOHN MALCOLM FRASER, PC, AC, CH. THERE IS A $500 REWARD FOR INFORMATION LEADING TO THE PUBLICATION OF THIS RARE, PERHAPS NON-EXISTENT, CULTURAL ARTIFACT.

Your editors amassed a considerable number of Paul Keating jokes during his ascendency to the Lodge and his incumbency. At the Australia Day ceremonials at Admiralty House in 1994, they were able to inform the then Prime Minister that exhaustive scholarship revealed that almost all the Keating jokes in circulation originally had been told about Hitler. Furthermore, the sources could be traced to two professional comedians working in Munich who were rewarded for their efforts by lengthy terms in Dachau.

Paul Keating entered a pub with a pig on a leash. He ordered two beers, one for him and one for the pig. After a couple of rounds, the barman's curiosity got the better of him.

'Where did you get him?' he asked.

'I won him in a raffle,' replied the pig.

Paul Keating visits the Canberra cemetery to negotiate a plot. He's taken with a grassy knoll, beside a eucalypt, with a splendid view. 'How much is this one?' he asks.

'Five thousand dollars,' says the cemetery official.

'Have you got anything cheaper?'

'Well, yes, there's one down the hill for $2000. But the view isn't very good.'

'Two thousand is still too much. What else have you got?'

'The only other plot we have is behind the tool shed.'

'How much is that?'

'Two hundred dollars. But, sir, an ex-Prime Minister of Australia can't be buried in a $200 plot.'

'No worries,' says Keating, 'I'm only going to be there three days.'

Paul Keating took his cabinet colleagues into the parliamentary dining room for dinner. The waiter approached the then prime minister and asked for his order.

Keating said: 'The steak.'

'Well done or rare?' asked the waiter.

'Rare,' said Keating.

'And what about the vegetables?' asked the waiter.

'They'll have what I have,' replied Keating.

POLITICIANS AWAY

Mr Dan Quayle landed at Sydney airport carrying a personal letter to Paul Keating from the President of the United States. Standing on the tarmac, he handed it to Keating as the photographers captured the moment. What did the letter say?

'Please ignore this man, he is an idiot.'

Bob Hawke visited

George Bush during the Gulf War and couldn't help but be impressed by the quality of the White House's staff. So he said to Bush: 'George, where do you get all these great staffers?'

Bush replied: 'It is very simple. Every morning I ask a staff member a trick question. Watch this – ' Bush then called for Dan Quayle. The VP walked in and Bush said: 'Dan, your mother has a child. It's not your brother, it's not your sister, who is it?'

Quayle replied: 'That's very simple, George. It's me.'

'Well done, Dan,' said the President, and Hawke was duly impressed. 'I've got to try that out.'

On his return to Canberra, he took his car straight into the office and put the same question to Paul Keating. 'Paul, your mother has a child. It's not your brother and it's not your sister. Who is it?'

Keating said: 'Gee, Bob, that's a tough one. I don't know the answer but I'll find out.' So he ran down to Johnny Button, well known as the brightest man in the government, and said: 'John, your mother has a child. It's not your brother, it's not your sister. So who is it?' Button looked at him, half took off his glasses like he always does, and said: 'Paul, you moron, it's me!'

Keating was delighted. 'Right! I've got it!' He ran back to Hawke and said: 'Bob, my mother has a child. It's not my brother and it's not my sister. But I know who it is.'

Hawke said: 'Well, who?'

Keating responded: 'John Button!'

Hawke looked at him and said: 'Don't be bloody silly, Paul. It's Dan Quayle!'

PROVIDED BY Senator William George (Bill) O'Chee, BA (Hons), Senator for Queensland since 1990.

Talleyrand once asked Napoleon: 'Why is it that your brothers hate you so much?'

After a pause, Napoleon said: 'They believe that I have robbed them of the inheritance of our late father, the King.'

THIS JOKE, if that's what it is, could only have come from Barry Jones. And it did. The Hon. Barry Owen Jones, AO, MA, LLB, DLitt, DSc, FTS, FAHA, FRSA and, currently, ALP National President. We're not sure what all those letters signify but FAHA does sound as though it might have something to do with telling jokes. Yet jokes are not Jones's milieu. In our experience he not only doesn't like telling them but he doesn't understand them when he hears them. The Talleyrand story, however, speaks volumes for Barry's notoriously eclectic scholarship.

There was a meeting between Bob Hawke, presidents Bush and Gorbachev. While they were discussing world problems the Angel of the Lord appeared to announce that God was not pleased and intended destroying the world in three weeks. Each travelled back to their respective country to make the announcement.

George told the Americans that he had good news and bad news. The good news being that he had proof of God's existence. The bad news was that God was going to pull the plug.

President Gorbachev told the Russians that he had bad news and worse news. The bad news was that God existed, despite Communist beliefs to the contrary, and the worse news was that the world was to be destroyed.

Bob Hawke, meanwhile, appeared on national television to tell us that he had good news and terrific news. Although he hadn't believed it previously, there really was a God. And the terrific news was that no child would be living in poverty in a month's time.

FROM THE WONDERFULLY christened Denver Beanland, one of a rapid succession of opposition leaders in Queensland.

Henry Kissinger was midway through one of his diplomatic marathons. He was sitting at the airport at Tel Aviv waiting for a jet to take him to a small but important sultanate. Oddly enough the airport terminal was all but deserted except for a rather serious-looking young Israeli who reminded Henry of Woody Allen.

'And what do you do, son?' enquired Henry, to pass the time.

'Oh, I've just passed my university course and I'm looking for a job,' said the boy. 'And what do you do?'

Though stunned by the boy's ignorance, Henry made a joke of it. 'Oh, I'm a sort of marriage broker.'

'Gee, do you think you could get me a good marriage?'

'Certainly. Just watch me.' Whereupon Henry had the airport officials contact the head of the Rothschild family in Paris. After a few pleasantries, Henry told Baron Rothschild that he had a young friend who'd be the perfect husband for his attractive daughter.

'Ah, Henry, everyone says that. Can you imagine how many suitors that girl has?'

'Ah, yes, but how many of her suitors represent David Rockefeller here in the Middle East?'

Whereupon Baron Rothschild agreed that the young man should press his suit.

Next Henry rang David Rockefeller in New York and said: 'David, I've got a young bloke here who wants to be your representative in the Middle East.'

David Rockefeller laughed. 'But Henry, there are hundreds of young men who want to be my representative in the Middle East.'

'Perhaps,' said Henry, 'but how many of them are engaged to Baron Rothschild's daughter?'

FROM THE SILVER BODGIE, aka the Hon. Robert James Lee Hawke, AC, BA, LLB, BLitt, Business Consultant, and Visiting Professor, University of Sydney. Hubby of Blanche.

Paul Keating, the Indian High Commissioner and the Israeli Ambassador are forced to seek emergency accommodation when their car breaks down in the middle of the bush. A farmer is happy to help, but has only two spare beds – 'So someone will have to sleep in the barn.'

WENDY MACHIN AGAIN.

The Israeli Ambassador volunteers. 'We Jewish people are used to sleeping in barns – it is part of our history.' But he returns to the house when he discovers that he'll be cohabiting with a pig, which just isn't kosher. Then the Indian High Commissioner steps forward, only to be knocking at the door a few minutes later, protesting the presence of a cow. 'The cow is sacred to us Indians,' he exclaims. 'I couldn't possibly sleep with one.' 'OK, scumbags,' says Paul, 'I'll go and sleep in the barn.' After five minutes there's another knocking on the door. The farmer opens it only to be confronted with the pig and the cow.

Saddam Hussein disappeared down

the bunker where he addressed his magic mirror, 'Magic mirror on the wall who is the biggest bastard of them all?'

The magic mirror said, 'Saddam Hussein, you are the biggest bastard of all.'

Saddam was so delighted with the response that he raced out and ordered a thousand of his faithful followers to be put to the sword.

The next week he disappeared down the bunker again. 'Magic mirror on the wall, who is the biggest bastard of all?'

'Saddam Hussein, you are still the biggest bastard of all.'

Saddam again was so delighted he declared war on the Kurds.

The next week he went into the bunker, but didn't return. His worried aides finally decided to seek him out. When they arrived there was Saddam crying uncontrollably in the corner.

'Sire, sire,' they cried, 'what's wrong?'

'Who's Paul Keating?' sobbed Saddam.

Stalin's corpse was having a very unsettling effect on Soviet citizenry, so Nikita rang President Kennedy and asked him if he'd help with his dilemma by taking Stalin's body. Kennedy said no, and suggested Khrushchev ring Macmillan. But Prime Minister Macmillan also refused, as did President de Gaulle. Khrushchev then called Ben Gurion of Israel and explained his problem. Ben Gurion said: 'Send it to us, we'll take care of it. But, remember, my country has the highest rate of resurrection in the world.'

PROFFERED BY the Hon. Andrew Sharp Peacock, LLB, whose ministerial duties included responsibility for Foreign Affairs in the Fraser government.

PART **Two**

The Laugh's on Others

BUSH & COUNTRY FOLK

A young man was collecting money around Wagga for the Murrumbidgee and Murray River Valley Drum and Fife Marching Band. He walked up a long path to a cottage and knocked. An old lady answered the door.

'Madam,' he said, 'I am taking up a collection for the Murrumbidgee and Murray River Valley Drum and Fife Marching Band and I thought you'd like to contribute.'

'What's that you say?' said the old dear, cupping her hands to her ear.

The young man raised his voice. 'Madam,' he shouted, 'I am collecting money for the Murrumbidgee and Murray River Valley Drum and Fife Marching Band and I thought you'd like to contribute.'

'You'll have to speak up,' yelled the old lady.

The young man took a deep breath and roared out: 'MADAM, I AM TAKING UP A COLLECTION FOR THE MURRUMBIDGEE AND MURRAY RIVER VALLEY DRUM AND FIFE MARCHING BAND AND I THOUGHT YOU MIGHT LIKE TO CONTRIBUTE.'

'I still can't get it,' yelled the old girl, her hands cupped to both ears. The young man gave up and started to walk down the path. As he did so the old lady called out, 'Don't forget to shut the gate.'

'Oh bugger the gate,' said the young man, all but under his breath.

'And bugger the Murrumbidgee and Murray River Valley Drum and Fife Marching Band,' yelled the old girl.

FROM LIFELONG APPARATCHIK to the Packer dynasty, David Ramsay McNicoll, CBE.

Thirty years ago, one of the fastest and most famous shearers in Australia was a bloke called Charlie Gibbs. Charlie shore all the 'long runs' between Queensland and NSW, shearing 200 a day, day after day, week after week, month after month. It was said of him that he was one of the very few shearers to have shorn 50 000 in a year.

Well, this story relates to an incident that occurred after Charlie arrived back in Bourke after a very long run.

As he walked into the hotel, the publican caught his eye and said: 'Charlie, there's a cocky just out of town who wants to know if you'll shear his sheep. Can you give him a ring?'

Charlie sauntered off to the telephone and rang the cocky.

'Oh, Mr Gibbs,' (cockies always call shearers 'Mister' before they shear the sheep), 'I heard your shed had cut out and was wondering if it would be possible for you to come and shear my sheep.'

'Oh, I suppose so,' said Charlie. 'How many have you got?'

'Three hundred and twelve,' replied the cocky.

There was a silence and Charlie said: 'What are their names?'

FROM THE LATE Michael Jerome Young, AO, whose Whitlam ministries included Immigration, Local Government and Ethnic Affairs and Multicultural Affairs. National President of the ALP during 1987–8, Mick was, in an earlier incarnation, a shearer. 'For many in politics,' wrote Bob Hawke, 'humour is a carefully crafted prop, but with Mick it was a spontaneous expression of his joy for life.'

Squatter Fraser was

exhibiting his prize bull at the annual Western District Agricultural Show as he did every year. Two hours before the judging he noticed the bull's eyes were crossed and knew that this would rule out any chance of a prize. He hurriedly called in the vet, who took one look at the beast and fished a plastic tube out of his black bag. The vet shoved one end of the tube into the bull's bum and blew vigorously through the other end. Instantly, the animal's eyes uncrossed and Squatter Fraser walked off with the blue ribbon.

At the following year's show, the same thing happened. Hoping to save a few bob, Fraser hunted around and found a piece of plastic tubing, knelt down and repeated the vet's routine. But the bull's eyes stayed firmly crossed. In desperation he called in the vet who quickly apprised himself of the situation, pulled the tube out of the bull's rectum, reversed it, pushed it in again and blew. Hey presto, the bull looked at the vet straight in the eye, but Squatter Fraser was puzzled. 'Tell me,' he asked the vet, 'why did you turn the tube around?' The vet regarded him with astonishment. 'You surely didn't think I'd be crazy enough to blow into the same end of the tube as an arsehole like you!'

JOAN COXSEDGE AGAIN.

A bloke was in court in the backblocks of Queensland charged with cattle duffing – taking somebody else's unbranded cattle and whacking his own brand on them.

The jury consisted of local farmers who'd all done a bit of duffing in their time, and the accused was a drinking mate from the Linga-Longa Pub. So when the judge sent them off to consider their verdict, their deliberations took about five minutes flat.

The clerk of the court said, 'Have you reached a verdict?'

'Yeah,' said the foreman of the jury.

'Do you find the defendant guilty or not guilty?'

'We reckon he's not guilty, but he's got to give the cattle back.'

The judge was infuriated and started banging away with his gavel. 'You cannot reach a verdict with such conditions attached! The man is either guilty or not guilty. Now go away and reconsider your verdict.'

The jury shuffled grumpily out of the court, only to return seconds later. 'Well!' said the judge. 'How do you find?'

'We find him not guilty, and he can keep the bloody cattle!'

THIS IS THE favourite joke of the Hon. Sir (Denis) James Killen, KCMG, LLB, Liberal minister extraordinaire. Jim tells us that it's based on an actual event in a Queensland court.

It's during the Depression when, late one evening in a country town, an old swaggie knocks on a lonely door. He hears footsteps approaching and the door opens, revealing a man with his collar back to front. The swaggie says: 'Oh, I'm terribly sorry to disturb you, Father.'

'I'm not a Father,' says the bloke, 'I'm a Church of England clergyman.'

'Whatever, I'll be on my way.'

'No, no. Come in, and tell me what I can do for you.'

Unused to religion, the swaggie's a bit shy. 'I don't want to come in. I'm going around seein' if I can get a meal in return for an odd job or two. I cut wood and stuff like that.'

The clergyman says: 'You are more than welcome. Sadly, I've just finished cutting our wood. However, if you'd care to stack it at the back of the house I'd be most pleased. And, of course, I'd give you a meal in exchange.'

So the swaggie stacks the wood, washes his hands and stands on the verandah at the back of the house. The clergyman insists that he enters, sitting him down at the kitchen table.

There's not much conversation during the meal. At the end of dinner, the swaggie says: 'Thanks Father, I'll be on my way.'

'No, no relax. Be comfortable. You can sleep out on the verandah tonight if you like.'

'Thanks very much, but I've got to be getting along.'

'Well then, before you go, let me pour you a cup of tea.'

The swaggie pours some into his saucer, blows on the surface and drinks it down. Meanwhile the clergyman has opened his *Bible* and is having a good read. The swaggie looks at him curiously and says: 'Must be a good book.'

The clergyman lifts his eyes and says: 'As a matter of fact, it's *the* good book.'

'Oh, yes. What's it about?'

'Surely you know what the *Bible* is about?'

'Well, I've *heard* of the *Bible*.'

'You've never read it?'

The swaggie's a bit embarrassed. 'Well, you see, I can't read.'

'That's nothing to be ashamed of, my man. That's why there are people like me involved in the church. We're able to read the word of God and pass it on to our less fortunate brethren.'

'Yeah, well, what's it about?'

'Well, it's about quite a number of things. All sorts of stories. Stories of the flood, of our Saviour. This particular part that I'm reading now is about an extremely powerful man of God. A man called Samson who came from a little town called Jerusalem. And he had a woman called Delilah. And these particular verses describe him joining Delilah in the fields whilst she was grinding the corn. Suddenly they were descended upon by 5000 Philistines. Samson called on God, picked up the jaw bone of an ass, slew 3000 of them and completely routed the rest.'

The swaggie looks at the minister in astonishment.

'And would this be a true story?'

'Of course it's true. It's the word of God.'

'He must have been a pretty strong sort of bloke.'

'Oh, an extremely powerful man. As a matter of fact, he was capable of tearing down temples with his bare hands. Simply by pushing over the pillars.'

'Fair dinkum?'

'How could it be anything else? It is, as I've emphasised, the word of God.'

'Yeah, I see.'

The following evening, late, the swaggie's looking for somewhere to camp and sees, in the middle distance, the glow of a campfire. He wanders up. Tentatively, observing the protocol of the bush, trying not to come too close.

Beside the campfire is an old rabbiter, brewing up a bunny stew in his four-gallon kero tin. He sees the swaggie in the shadows and says: 'G'day. Come and get warm and help yourself to the stew.'

The swaggie hops into the bunny stew very appreciatively and the rabbiter says: 'What do you know?'

'Oh, nothing much. Oh yeah, I did hear something. Terrible story. About this bloke called Simpson. Simpson from Jerilderie. A real bastard. He's going around ripping up the telephone poles. It turns out he was out in the paddock one day giving his girlfriend Delicious a grind in the corn when, all of a sudden, 5000 Filipino bastards appeared. So he picks up the arse-bone of a Jew, slays 3000 and completely roots the rest. Turned out to be a bit of a poofter.'

JACK THOMPSON. From his own lips, on a refuse-littered roof, masquerading as a rooftop garden, of a battered Beijing hotel during time off from a cultural delegation co-starring David Williamson and Noni Hazlehurst. Not simply told but performed to Oscar-nomination standard.

Bush & Country Folk

Once upon a time, way out past the back of Bourke, two grizzled old drovers were leaning on the bar of the local pub, discussing the relative merits of various dogs. 'Now, I reckon my Blue Heeler's the smartest dog in the country,' said one, '. . . do anythin' that it's told.'

'Nah,' said the other, 'me Kelpie's master – 'e thinks for 'imself.'

They argued back and forth across the mounting pile of empty glasses, the yarns about what each dog could do getting wilder and more far-fetched. But neither could agree with the other.

'Tell you what,' one said, 'Let's put it to the test. Meet you out by the chicken run termorrer mornin'.'

Morning rose bright and early. The two codgers rose bluff and bleary, and went out to the chicken run with their dogs.

'Right, Bluey,' said the bloke with the Heeler. 'Now you listen here and you listen good, coz I'm only gonna tell yer once.' The dog sat and watched him, eyes bright and ears erect. 'Now Blue, I want yer ter go down that road fer about a mile and yer'll come ter a gate. Go through the gate, up over the hill, ter yer left and yer'll come ter a brick wall with another gate. Open the gate, go through and yer'll find three poddy calves. Round up the calves, bring 'em through the gate, close it, bring 'em back over the hill, through the second gate and back here. Yer got that?' The dog barked, wheeled, scampered off down the road, through the gate, over the hill, got the calves, closed the gate, over the hill, through the gate, closed it, and brought the calves back to his master.

'Geez, that's pretty smart,' said the bloke with the Kelpie, but that's nothin'. You watch this... Oi, Kelly! Breakfast!'

The dog looked around, dashed off down the road, came back with a billy of water, collected some sticks, begged a Vesta off his master, lit the fire, put the billy on to boil, scrabbled his way under the wire of the chicken coop, collected an egg, put it in the water, sat and watched it for three and a half minutes, took the billy off the fire, gently tipped the egg out at the bloke's feet, then stood on its head.

'Geez, that's bloody clever,' said the bloke with the Heeler, 'but what's the silly bugger doing standin' on 'is 'ead?'

'Ah!' said the other bloke, ''e's not so silly. 'e knows I haven't got an eggcup.'

THIS JOKE WAS submitted by many people, in many forms. The most classic interpretation, however, came from the late Mick Young.

Bush & Country Folk

The Australian hayseeds, Dad and Dave, first appeared as characters in On Our Selection *by Steele Rudd. The Rudd stories were turned into films by the veteran Australian director, Ken Hall, with a very young Peter Finch playing Dave. The sexual escapades of Dave and Mabel have been a staple of Australian humour ever since, with most jokes focusing on the two innocents dealing with the wickedness of the big city. A familiar theme in Australian popular culture, it was recently recycled for the Crocodile Dundee films.*

Dad and Dave were standing watching a dingo licking its privates. Dave said to Dad: 'Just between you and me, I've wanted to do that all my life.'

Dad said: 'Go ahead, but I'd pat him a bit first. He looks pretty vicious to me.'

Dave returned to Snake Gully after a brief trip to Europe.

Dad said: 'Reckon you saw a lot of mighty fine things in Europe.'

'Sure did, Dad. Cathedrals, palaces, mansions. But what impressed me most were the dunnies. They sure have got terrific dunnies. And they all flush.'

'Well, son,' said Dad, 'reckon you ought to build yourself one of those posh dunnies. But you'll have to get rid of the old shithouse first.'

'Nothing to it, Dad.' Dave took out a hand grenade that he happened to have on him, pulled out the pin and threw it at the shithouse.

Dad's a slow thinker and a slow mover. After a while he said: 'I don't reckon you should have done that, son.'

Out of the debris staggered Mum. She lurched up to Dad and said: 'Reckon it must have been something I ate.'

Dave and Mabel were out walking along the river bank one Sunday afternoon, when they came across Herb Wilson sitting by a large tree with a fishing line in the river.

'Are yer catchin' any?' asked Dave.

'Just a few,' said Herb.

'How big?'

'Just tiddlers,' said Herb, 'about the size of your diddle.'

Dave and Mabel retreated to the other side of the tree and started to have a cuddle. Shortly after, Mabel called out to Herb. 'Eh! Herb,' she called.

'Yes Mabel.'

'I'll bet yer catchin' some whoppers, now.'

Mum is working in the kitchen when Dad enters with his first erection in years. 'Mum...get into bed,' he says.

She takes off her apron, puts all the ingredients and utensils away, washes her hands, gets into bed...but too late. Dad has withered away.

'Ya know...we can't 'ave this 'appen agin,' says Dad. 'Next time I git one of these, I'll ring the firebell so you start gittin' ready when youse hears it. When I git to the house, we'll be right.'

A year goes by. Mum's in the kitchen. She hears the firebell. She goes through all the preparations. Dad comes pounding into the house, through the kitchen, into the bedroom where Mum lies waiting for him. He looks at her and says: 'Get up, yer oversexed fool...the barn's on fire!'

PROFESSIONAL CARERS

Q. What's the difference between a Rottweiler and a social worker?

A. The Rottweiler eventually gives the child back.

FROM JOAN KIRNER, then Premier of Victoria. She told this joke when a large number of kids were seized from parents who belonged to a US religious cult. The joke proved to be as controversial as the police action, and the subsequent court case.

Q. Why is psychoanalysis a lot quicker for a man than for a woman?

A. When it's time to go back to his childhood he's already there.

A patient recently came into a psychiatrist's office and told him he had a major problem. When the doctor asked him what the problem was, the man said: 'Well, some mornings I wake up and think I'm a tee-pee. Other mornings I wake up and think I'm a wigwam.'

The psychiatrist responded immediately: 'I know exactly what your problem is.'

'Well, doc, what is it?'

'You're too tense.'

PROFFERED BY THE Hon. Peter Thomas Anderson, ex-Minister for Police and Emergency Services, erstwhile radio announcer and currently member of the Police Board.

Two psychiatrists, Dick and Harry, meet twenty years after graduation. Dick says he feels burnt out and depressed and is thinking of early retirement.

Harry: 'Let's see. I've got three questions which I try out on my patients to see what shape they're in. Why don't I run them past you, and see how bad it really is?'

Dick: 'All right.'

Harry: 'First, what does a man do standing up, a woman do sitting down, and a dog do on three legs?'

Dick: 'That's easy ... shake hands.'

Harry: 'Right. Second question. What does a dog do in your backyard which, when you step in it, causes you to utter an expletive?'

Dick: 'That's obvious ... digs a hole.'

Harry: 'That's right too. Finally, where do women have the curliest hair?'

Dick: 'I know. In Fiji.'

Harry: 'Right. Look, there's nothing whatever wrong with you. But you should hear the bizarre answers I get from some of my patients.'

A psychiatrist was concerned that too many of his professional clients seemed incapable of making a decision. To demonstrate this inability he devised a simple experiment. His first patient was a civil engineer. When asked what 2 + 2 made, the engineer fumbled in his pocket, operated the slide rule and, after some manipulation, looked up in a puzzled way and said: '3.98. No, that doesn't seem right, I'll try again.' Becoming more and more agitated, he thought it might be 4.01.

The next client was a physician of some distinction, and he was posed the same question. What he said was: 'I think it's probably 4, but it could possibly be something else. Perhaps we'd better refer the matter to a specialist.'

The lawyer client, who was next, thought that, in general, it would be considered 4, but that they should have counsel's opinion.

The psychiatrist's last patient was an accountant who, when asked the question 'What does 2 + 2 make?', looked him straight in the eye and said: 'What do you want it to make?'

FROM GORDON BRYANT, the amiable ex-Member for Wills and member of the Whitlam ministry. A similar version sporting a politician in the punchline was supplied by the Hon. Bruce George Baird, BA, MBA.

Two psychiatrists pass in a corridor. 'Good morning,' said the first. The second walked on wondering, 'I wonder what he meant by that?'

A doctor was doing his hospital rounds with an Irish nurse. When he came to one bed he pronounced, 'Nurse, this patient has died.'

The old fellow in the bed said, 'I'm all right. I'm not dead!'

The nurse responded, 'Will you be quiet? The doctor knows best.'

An old bloke, over 90, was brought into Alice Springs for a medical. It was a regular, yearly trip made by his daughter and her husband from their cattle property about 100 km out of Alice, and the old bloke was getting a bit forgetful.

Their regular doctor got him to strip and they went through all the tests. Tap tap, cough, take a deep breath, stick your tongue out, all the usual stuff. The old bloke was all sunburnt on his face and hands but the rest of him was bluish white, semi-transparent. You could have held him up to the window if you'd wanted to check the state of his organs.

'Well, Mr Quinn,' said the doctor, 'you are in remarkable physical condition for a man of your age. There's just one more test. But you probably remember the routine from last time.'

The old man said, with a shaky voice, 'how do you mean "routine"?'

'Well, you'll remember that we went through all these tests last year.'

'I've never seen you before in my life,' was his quavering response.

'I assure you you have. But no matter.' The doctor pointed to a shelf containing an array of different-shaped beakers and said: 'It just remains for you to fill one of those bottles with a sample of your urine.'

'What?' said the old fella, pointing with a shaking hand across the room. 'From *here*?'

ROLF HARRIS. Rolf shares more of his reputation-enhancing wit on later pages.

A man went to a doctor to have his eyes tested.

'Put your left hand over your right eye and read the top line of the chart,' said the doctor.

The man put his right hand over his left eye.

'No, put your LEFT hand over your RIGHT eye and just read the top line of the chart,' said the doctor.

The man put his left hand over his left eye.

'No,' said the doctor, 'put your LEFT HAND over your RIGHT EYE and just read the letters on the top line of the bloody chart.'

The man put his right hand over his right eye.

'Oh, for Chrissake,' said the doctor and he grabbed a cardboard box, cut a small hole where the man's left eye would be and fitted the box over the man's head.

'Now read me the top line of that chart,' he said.

There was a muffled soft sobbing sound coming from inside the cardboard box.

'Oh, my God,' said the doctor, 'what's wrong now?'

'Well, what I really wanted,' said the man, 'was a pair of those little ROUND glasses like John Lennon.'

RECEIVED FROM John Morrison Clarke, mild-mannered genius from Palmerston North, New Zealand, whose contribution to Australian letters, broadcasting and cinema in a variety of personas, including Fred Dagg, has endeared him to our grateful nation.

MONEY-BROKERS & MONEY-SPENDERS

An economist is a person who marries Elle Macpherson for her money.

THIS WAS TOLD by John Hewson at the University of New South Wales Open Day, September 1992. Readers may recall that John Robert Hewson, BEcon (Hons Syd.), MA, PhD, was, briefly, a leader of the Liberal Party. As well as jokes about economists, he also told people about the GST but, sadly, nobody laughed.

Two beautiful girls were walking down St George's Terrace when they heard a cry for help. They had some trouble working out where it was coming from, but eventually found a green frog sitting on a window ledge. The frog was in a pretty emotional state and explained that it had been a Perth entrepreneur. He had fallen under the spell of the NCSC and been turned into a green frog. Only one thing could save him. To be kissed by a beautiful girl.

The girls seemed rather doubtful about his approach but he assured them that he was, truly, a Perth entrepreneur, and he promised them anything, and indeed everything, if one of them would only kiss him and restore him to his previous condition. The girls looked at him for a while. Suddenly one of them opened her handbag, picked up the frog, dropped him inside and snapped it shut. 'Good heavens,' said her friend, 'what are you doing?'

'Well,' said the girl with the handbag, 'I'm no fool. I know that a talking frog is worth a lot more than a Perth entrepreneur.'

A FAVOURITE JOKE of the Hon. Frederick Michael Chaney, LLB. Another Lib. with ambitions to lead his party, Fred turned out to be too liberal for the Liberals. Alienated by the way politics is practised in Western Australia, Fred is no longer a practising politician.

A very rich and respected Toorak lady held a tea party for her rich and influential friends, and ate more cucumber sandwiches than was good for her.

During one of those deadly silences that happen in even the best of parties, a colossal breaking of wind came from the hostess's direction. Never one to be easily embarrassed, she quickly said to her butler, 'James, stop that immediately!'

The butler turned slowly and replied in his most superior voice, 'Certainly madam, which way did it go?'

A wealthy and unusually idealistic merchant banker was pottering around the backyard of his mansion one day when an itinerant handyman came around and asked him for a bit of casual work. Feeling sorry for the fellow, the banker produced five litres of enamel paint and a brush and told the handyman he would like him to go and paint the front porch.

An hour later the handyman was around the back again to collect his earnings. The banker commended him on the speed of his work and handed him ten dollars. As he was leaving the handyman remarked, 'By the way, it's not a Porsche, it's a Mercedes.'

A bloke walked into a bank and joined a very long queue. Finally he made it to a teller and asked for an appointment with the bank's manager.

The teller apologised. 'Sadly, the bank manager passed away last week.'

Whereupon the man thanked her and rejoined the still lengthy queue, only to be given the same message by the second teller.

He then joined the long queue yet again, finally putting the same question to the third teller, who protested, 'But I just overheard my colleague explaining to you that the bank manager recently passed away!'

The gentleman thanked him but explained he just liked hearing the good news.

During a divorce case in Adelaide, many years ago, the woman complainant, who was not represented by legal counsel, told the judge that she knew her husband had committed adultery.

'How do you know?' the judge asked.

FROM THE HON. Donald Allan Dunstan, AC, LLB, famous chef and ex-Premier of South Australia.

The woman replied that her husband had contracted Venetian disease.

The judge queried: 'And what is Venetian disease, may I ask?'

The woman looked flustered, but counsel for the defendant stood up and said: 'I think she means a case of gondoliers, Your Honour.'

A lawyer working for the family court forgot that he was due at a divorce settlement. By the time he arrived he saw his Aboriginal client, a woman, leaving the court holding a sheet of rusty galvanised iron.

'I'm terribly sorry I wasn't here in time,' he said.

'It's okay,' said the woman, 'I managed fine without you. Look, I got half the house.'

Q. What do you call a bigot in a wig?

A. Your Honour.

①

Q. What do you call a few hundred bigots in wigs?

A. The Australian judicial system.

①

Q. What do you call a judge driving through a working-class suburb?

A. Lost.

①

Q. Have you heard about the Australian judge who got confused?

A. He was prejudiced in favour of a woman.

CREATIVE INDUSTRY TYPES

David Hill is going to work one day and he gets in the David Hill lift and goes up to the David Hill suite. The lift makes an unscheduled stop on the third floor and in walks a very attractive blonde who David has never seen before. The woman obviously doesn't work for the ABC because she is not carrying anything in triplicate.

She and David look at each other and she says: 'David Hill?'

And he says: 'Yes.'

And she says: 'I'd like to give you a blow job.'

And this is the mark of the man. David Hill looks at her and says: 'Yes . . . fine. But what's in it for me?'

TOLD BY Andrew Denton at a major ribbon-cutting ceremony at the ABC's new studios in Ultimo, in the presence of its central character. Exhaustive scholarship by your editors reveals that the joke had an American pre-incarnation, with Donald Trump as the fellated celebrity.

David Hill and his wife were in bed today.

'God...' she said, to which he responded, 'You may call me David when we're in bed.'

In the heady days of the 10BA tax concessions, almost everyone in Australia seemed to be making a movie. Every accountant, solicitor and tax consultant was packaging the films on behalf of clients who would enjoy the 150 per cent write-off designed to boost local production.

One of them was a local solicitor with a modest practice in conveyancing. Very excitedly, he approached a prospective investor.

'I've got the most marvellous film on the go. It's going to make a fortune. The script is by Carey.'

The prospective investor was mightily impressed. '*Peter* Carey?'

'No, Gavin Carey. He's a member of our Rotary branch. But it's being directed by Weir.'

'*Peter* Weir?'

'No, Bill Weir. You know Bill, works as a surveyor for the local council. But the cinematographer's McAlpine.'

'*Don* McAlpine?'

'No, Harry McAlpine. You know, the bloke in the arcade who does weddings and bar mitzvahs. And Smeaton is doing the music.'

'*Bruce* Smeaton?'

'No, not Bruce. Arthur. The Uniting Church's organist.'

The would-be investor heaved a heavy sigh. 'And who have you got producing?'
'The McElroy brothers.'
'Hal and Jim?'
'Yes!'

A CLASSIC 'IN-JOKE' providing an inventory of luminaries in the Australian film industry. The unfortunate targets of the story, Hal and Jim McElroy, are amongst Australia's most fecund and ubiquitous producers. This joke was submitted by— who, in the interests of his career, wishes this to be a closely guarded secret.

Lord Olivier arrived in heaven. 'Who are you?' asked St Peter.

'I'm Laurence Olivier, the world's greatest actor, poet and playwright,' came the reply.

'Well,' said St Peter, 'let's look at the Great Register.' He opened the book and started thumbing through. 'Olivier... Fred, Olivier... Jim, Olivier... Laurence... Yes! Here we are! Well, your instructions are to follow that pathway over there until you come to a vine-covered English cottage in which you'll find Lord Byron and William Shakespeare.'

'Right,' said Lord Olivier, and set off. Pretty soon he found the cottage and knocked on the door.

'Come in,' said a voice, 'and identify yourself.' Lord Olivier entered. 'I'm Laurence Olivier, the world's greatest actor, poet and playwright.'

'Aha,' replied Byron, 'I'd heard about the actor and playwright bit – but the world's greatest poet? Indeed, Shakespeare and I would contest that point.'

'Indeed we would,' agreed Shakespeare. 'So why not a small rhyming competition to settle the argument once and for all?'

'I agree,' said Olivier.

'Me too,' said Byron, 'but what shall we rhyme about?'

'How about a bow-legged man standing by a river?' suggested Shakespeare.

'OK with me,' said Olivier, 'I'll go first.

Down where the mighty river flowed
There stood a man whose legs were bowed.'

'Very good,' said Byron, 'but methinks far too simple. Try this!

Where the river to the sea comes out
Stands there a man with legs about.'

'Excellent, Byron,' said Shakespeare, 'but I'm sure I can do better than both those... listen!

Sooth, what manner of man is this
Whose balls hang in parenthesis?'

Just then Banjo Paterson happened to be walking past their window. He stuck his head in and said:

'Well! I've copped some lurks and seen some rackets.
But a bastard, with his balls in brackets!?'

SUBMITTED BY SOMETIMES broadcaster and long-term archivist of local humour Phil Haldeman.

Wilde was reclining, as was his wont, in velour smoking jacket, carnation in button hole, vellum-bound volume of poetry in hand, in his undergraduate rooms, when he heard a great clatter on the stairs below and a door burst open to reveal eight hearty and perspiring rugger players manifestly bent on disturbing his repose.

Wilde rose to his feet and surveyed the scene in a dignified but slightly nervous manner. 'I say chaps,' he said, 'I may be inverted, but I'm not insatiable.'

GARETH EVANS'S FAVOURITE anecdote-joke which he heard during his stay at Magdalen College. Evans speculates that Fraser heard the joke too 'except that Fraser no doubt got it from the rugger-buggers whereas I, of course, got it from the aesthetes'.

RELIGIOUS BEINGS

Moses went back up the mountain. 'Excuse me, God, I just want to get this straight. The Arabs get all the oil, and we get to cut the ends off our what????'

A novice went to a monastery where the monks were only allowed to speak two words a year, and those to the abbot. At the end of each year they were given an audience and said their two words. Naturally they were expected to be something along the lines of 'Jesus loves' or some other eternal verity. However at the end of his first year the novice offered, 'Bed hard' and at the end of the second year, 'Food bad' and at the end of the third year his two words were, 'I quit'.

'I'm not surprised,' said the abbot, 'you've done nothing but whinge ever since you came here.'

During the brief, distinguished reign of Pope John XXIII, a young priest riding his bike in New York was stopped at the traffic lights and saw Christ walking across the pedestrian crossing. Excited by the sight, he rode feverishly to the cathedral and reported the incident to the Monsignor. The Monsignor said: 'This is too big for me to handle – you'll have to speak to the Cardinal.'

The Cardinal was then informed of the incident and said: 'This is too big for me to handle – I shall have to ring Rome.'

So the Cardinal got out the green phone, dialled Vat 69 and spoke to the Pope. He said to the Holy Father: 'We have a dreadful problem in New York. Christ is here and he's coming to the cathedral. What are we going to do?'

There was no reply from the Pope, just heavy breathing.

The Cardinal then said: 'Your Holiness, you'll have to advise us. He will be here at the cathedral in a few minutes.'

There was another long silence at the end of the line. Finally the Pope said: 'You betta lookka very bizzi – '

FROM ERSTWHILE Senator the Hon. John Norman Button, BA, LLB, now enjoying life as an author, columnist and corporate adviser.

All the cardinals gather in the Sistine Chapel to elect a new Pope. An assassin plants a bomb and all are killed instantly. So the eighty of them arrive at the Pearly Gates *en masse*. As they're strolling in, Peter stops them and says, 'Where do you think you're going?'

'We have come to collect our eternal reward,' they chorus, 'we are princes of the church.'

'Well, nobody gets straight in without answering this question. Have you committed adultery?'

Suddenly the cardinals look very sheepish and confused. Then, one by one, they shuffle outside the gates leaving only a single cardinal within.

'Okay, okay,' says Peter to the seventy-nine cardinals. 'Away you go to Purgatory for twelve months. And take that deaf bastard with you.'

A nun is in the shower when there's a loud banging at the convent door. All the other nuns are out the back, in the garden.

'Who is it?' she calls out.

'I'm the blind man from the village,' is the reply.

So she runs downstairs in the nude and opens the door.

'Great knockers,' says the visitor. 'Where do you want the blinds?'

St Peter was talking to the Virgin Mary. 'And what's it like being mother of the world's most talked-about prophet?'

The Virgin replied: 'Well, actually, we were hoping he'd become a doctor.'

FROM DAVID HILL, MEcon, quiet, self-effacing managing director of the Australian Broadcasting Corporation from 1986 to 1995.

PART **Three**
Political(ly) Incorrect

RACISM

FROM ERSTWHILE Senator John Button, yet again.

A Russian official woke Mr Brezhnev one morning saying: 'Comrade Brezhnev, I'm sorry to wake you, but there are two very important items of news which you'll have to know about. One of them is good and one is bad. Which do you want to hear first?'

Brezhnev said: 'I'd better hear the bad news first.'

The official said: 'Comrade Brezhnev, the Chinese have landed on the moon.'

Brezhnev said: 'God, that's awful. What's the good news?'

'All of them,' said the official.

Two white men and an Aborigine were in prison together. One of the whites said he was in for ten years for attempted rape, but thought himself lucky he hadn't actually done the rape or he would be in for twenty years.

The other white said he was in for fifteen years for attempted murder, but was lucky his victim had lived, or he would be doing life.

The Aborigine then said he was in for twenty-five years for riding his bike without a light, but reckoned he was lucky it wasn't night time.

A New Zealand minister had been forced to resign, and while he was packing up he looked out the window of his office, high above the streets of Wellington, and said to his staff: 'See that new school over there? Well, last year I persuaded cabinet to vote for the money for that school. Yes, I built that school. But do you think the voters will remember me for that?

'And see that new hospital down the street? Well, the year before I built the school I had to call in every political debt owed me to get cabinet to back that hospital. But I did it. And I built that hospital. But will the voters ever remember me for that? Course they bloody won't!

'And see that six-lane freeway out to the airport? Well, the first year I was a minister, the year after we just managed to win the election, I had to squeeze cabinet like you wouldn't believe to get the money for that, and I built that freeway, and you can bet the voters won't ever give me a second thought for that either.

'But screw one sheep and they never forget!'

FROM SENATOR THE HON. Robert Lindsay (Bob) Collins, Federal Minister for Primary Industries and Energy in the Hawke and Keating governments, and one of the best stand-up comics in the Upper House.

An aristocratic family in Delhi sent their favourite son to Harvard, whence he returned with that most desirable of degrees, an MBA. Determined to demonstrate his managerial brilliance, he approached the government with a brilliant idea. To raise money for the Indian Treasury he will conduct, on their behalf, the biggest lottery in the history of the world. The entire population of India will be encouraged to buy tickets. Although each will pay only a few rupees, the amount of money raised will be immense.

The ticket sales go very well. Finally comes the day of the draw. The young man with the MBA has arranged for all the ticket stubs to be deposited in a vast wooden barrel which is positioned high above the swelling crowds, on an elaborately carved platform. And on the platform – many of India's most famous political and cultural celebrities. A magnificently painted elephant has been trained to turn the barrel, so that the stubs are properly mixed, and India's most beauteous film star is on hand to call out the winning numbers. The entire event is to be compered by the young 'MBA', whilst the actual prize will be read out by India's Treasurer.

At the appointed time the crowd has grown to immense proportions, stretching from one end of India to the other.

The elephant churns the barrel and the movie star is asked to pull out the number of the third prize winner. The 'MBA' proclaims the number through his microphone, his voice echoing through thousands and thousands of loudspeakers strung up lamp posts, trees and minarets. Finally there is a response from far, far away in the crowd and a thin figure in a dhoti is seen weaving his way through the multitude crying: 'It's me, it's me!'

Finally he arrives breathless on the platform. The Treasurer announces the third prize. 'You have won two first-class airline tickets from Air India to take you anywhere you wish around the world, along with 1000 English pounds spending money.'

The crowd goes wild.

Now the elephant churns the mighty barrel and the sequence is repeated for the second prize. This time the winner has to run even further, almost all the way from Jaipur.

'Congratulations,' says the Treasurer, 'you have won second prize. Here it is, this beautiful fruit cake.'

The little Indian chap is very upset. 'A fruit cake? But the third prize was airline tickets and lots of money.'

Attempting to soothe the indignant prizewinner the 'MBA'

explains, 'But this is no ordinary fruit cake...this fruit cake was baked...' and he takes a deep breath as he makes the proud announcement '...by Madam Gandhi!'

To which the prizewinner responds: 'Fuck Madam Gandhi!'

'Ah no no no,' says the 'MBA', with a characteristically Indian shake of the head, 'that is first prize!'

THE AFOREMENTIONED, foreword-mentioned Bob Hawke frequently told the foregoing joke at fund-raising functions during his ascendency to power. Unfortunately he chose to recycle it for a major Labor Party occasion when the audience of party faithful was augmented by many from Canberra's diplomatic community. The joke was hissed at for sexism and booed for racism and proved deeply offensive to the Indian High Commissioner. For a time it seemed that the outraged response to the story had destroyed Hawke's political career. The joke must have continued to haunt him as PM, particularly after Gandhi's assassination, or when he dealt with her son Rajiv at gatherings of Commonwealth prime ministers. The lesson contained in this story was lost on the likes of Arthur Tunstall, Alexander Downer and, more recently, Dr Brendan Nelson, all of whom have damaged their prospects by telling politically incorrect jokes.

The Italian-Australian retired from his factory job. He went to the nearest chicken hatchery and said, 'I ama retiring to open a chicken farma. Please sella me 10 000 day-olda chicks.' He took delivery and went on his way.

Three days later he approached the hatchery sales clerk again. 'I wanna 10 000 day-olda chicks.' He took delivery and went on his way.

Three days later he was back at the counter. 'I wanna 10 000 day-olda chicks.'

The salesperson enquired, 'You certainly have bought a lot of chicks. Have you got a very large farm?'

The old man replied, 'No, all the others died. I think I might be planting them too deep.'

A grid-iron football match in Boston. A vociferous lady with a strong Irish accent on the fence, giving her views. As the opposing scrums inclined together for battle, she shouted: 'Give the ball to Muldoon!'

A wild scuttle, the ball emerged, and was slung to a player. He was borne down by a pride of opponents and carried off on a stretcher. His replacement ran on. Still the lady shouted: 'Give the ball to Muldoon!'

Another scrum. Again the ball passed to a player who was promptly flung heavily to the ground and was assisted, limping, from the arena. As his substitute ran on the lady still shouted: 'This time, give the ball to Muldoon!'

A figure stood up in the scrum, cupped his hands and shouted back: 'Muldoon say he don't want the ball!'

OFFERED BY THE Hon. Sir Rupert James Hamer, AC, KCMG, a popular, genuinely liberal Liberal premier. Bearing as much similarity to Jeff Kennett as a chrysanthemum to a cactus.

Racism 101

When I was flying to Singapore I asked the man sitting next to me where he was going. His reply was:

'DDDDDDDDDUUUUUUUUBBBBBBBBBLLLLLLLLIIIIINNNNN.'

I then asked what he was going to do in Dublin. His reply was that he was going to Dublin 'TTTTTTOOOOO BBBBBBEEEEE AAAAAAAA RRRRRRAAAAACCCCCIIIIINNNN NGGGGGGG BBBBRRRRROOOOAAAADDDDD CCCCAAAAASSSSTTTEEEEERRRRR'.

I asked him if he really expected to get the job. 'NNNNNNOOOOO. They'll probably give it to a bloody Catholic.'

FROM THE HON. Brian James Dixon, BComm, DipEd, MACE who went from the football field to parliament becoming a minister for this and that in the Hamer government. He is probably best known, however, for commissioning the Life. Be In It campaign, starring Norm, from Phillip Adams and Alex Stitt.

102 Political(ly) Incorrect

Paddy finally got the job and went along on his first day. He was given his chainsaw and told he must cut down twenty trees to earn his wages. He returned in the evening tired out.

'How many did you cut today, Paddy?'

'Five.'

'Sorry, no wages today.'

Next day, 'How many today, Paddy?'

'Ten.'

'Sorry Paddy, not enough.'

On the third day, Paddy crawls into the office.

'How many today, Paddy?'

'Fifteen, sir, and it's the best I can do.'

The foreman shook his head. 'I don't understand it. The others all reach their quota. Perhaps there's something wrong with your saw.' He took the chainsaw, started it up.

Paddy leapt back in horror. 'What's that noise?'

Q. Why wasn't Jesus Christ born in Australia?

A. Because they couldn't find three wise men and a virgin.

①

Q. Why do Aussies put XXXX on a can of beer?

A. They can't spell 'beer'.

①

Q. What's the difference between an Aussie and a Qantas jet?

A. The jet stops whining when it gets to England.

①

Q. Why is racist abuse like pooing your own pants?

A. Because you only do it when you're really scared.

SEXISM

Wally loved Wendy, so he decided to prove it by having her name tattooed on his penis for her birthday. After dinner, he showed it to her in all its glory. WENDY, tattooed along the length of it.

Wendy thought it was beaut. Even when it was detumescent and all you could see was WY.

Later on, Wally was in a public loo when he noticed that the bloke peeing beside him also had WY tattooed on his dick. Wally was at once suspicious and curious. 'Is your girlfriend's name Wendy?'

'No,' said the other bloke, 'I've never had a sheila called Wendy. Why?'

'Well, it's your tattoo,' said Wally as he rather shyly revealed his own.

'Great,' said the bloke. 'Very impressive.'

'You can only see WY,' said Wally, 'but when I get an erection it says WENDY. What does yours say?'

'Well, it's a bit of a mouthful. It says WELCOME TO WOOLLOOMOOLOO AND HAVE A NICE DAY.'

Q. What do you call the useless piece of skin on the end of a penis?

A. A man.

Senator John Button was staying at a hotel in Los Angeles where there was a convention of comic book superheroes – Batman, Spiderman, Wonderwoman, etc. A Button breakfast was interrupted by the arrival of Superman, who said he was feeling the worse for wear after a heavy night. Button enquired what had taken place. Superman said that he'd come back to his room after a party and was preparing for bed when his x-ray vision revealed that Wonderwoman was lying naked in the next room. Superman said he could do nothing else but crash through the wall, landing on the bed. So Button said to Superman: 'Well, that must have surprised Wonderwoman!' To which Superman replied: 'Not nearly as much as it surprised the Invisible Man!'

INCREDIBLY, THIS STORY was proffered by the Hon. John Cain, ex-Premier of Victoria, generally regarded as somewhat humourless. John submitted this joke, previously told by Senator Button at an ALP fundraiser, reporting that it provoked a similar response to Hawke's Madam Gandhi joke. Button, it seems, was roundly abused by a number of female comrades for 'sexism'.

Bruce returned home late, after boozing with his mates. The house was in darkness. He undressed in the lounge and, as he slipped into bed, remembered that he'd been neglecting his wife of late. Later, he went to the bathroom to clean his teeth and was astonished to find his wife in the bathtub reading a book.

'What the hell are you doing here?' he said.

'What's wrong with relaxing in the bath?'

'Nothing. But who the hell is that in our bed?'

'I told you that my mother was coming to stay!'

At this, Bruce slammed the door, went back to the bedroom and screamed at the recumbent figure, 'Why the hell didn't you tell me it was you!'

'How could I, Bruce, when we haven't been on speaking terms for years?'

A tough-looking bloke turned up at the red light district in Kalgoorlie and said to the Madam: 'Give us the roughest sheila you've got.'

Pretty soon he's ensconced with a great big brassy-looking blonde, and, as she slips her dressing gown off, he strikes a wax match right across her breasts and lights a cigar. He's pleased that she doesn't seem surprised or at all concerned. So he turns away from her with a grin and proceeds to rip off his gear. When he's finished, he turns around, still puffing away, and finds her with her back to him, bent double, clutching both her ankles.

'What are you doing?' he says.

She casually replies: 'I just thought you might like to open a bottle of beer before we get started.'

①

'Am I the first girl you ever made love to?'

'You might be. Were you around the back of Rushcutters Bay Stadium at the Everly Brothers' concert in 1960?'

①

Sheila and Bruce have not been practising safe sex. While Bruce never takes his socks off, he is disinclined to wear a condom. Now the poor girl discovers that she's pregnant and says: 'If you don't marry me, I'm going to jump off Sydney Harbour Bridge.' Bruce's reply is a fond slap on the back. 'You're not only a great root, you're also a good sport!'

SADLY, THE LAST three jokes are all from the Paderewski of the wobble board, Rolf Harris, AM, OBE, MBE. Tsk, tsk.

Four mates were playing golf. One of them was bending over a putt, concentrating like mad, when a funeral procession passed by on a nearby road.

He straightened up, removed his hat, held it over his breast and remained at silent attention until the cortège had passed. His three mates were amazed. They'd never known him to be a man of particular sensitivity and praised him for his respect for the dead.

'It's the least I could do,' he said modestly, 'we would have been married twenty-eight years tomorrow.'

A businessman was faced with the dilemma of firing two of his three secretaries. All were good at their jobs, and he didn't know how he was going to choose between them. Finally he decided to put an extra $100 in each of their pay envelopes and judge their reactions.

The first secretary surreptitiously pocketed the extra money and didn't say a word. The second came to him and said, 'Look, I've been overpaid $100, so I went out and invested it in bonds at twelve-and-a-half per cent.' And the third secretary came to him and said, 'Look, I was overpaid $100. It's not mine. I haven't earnt it. I want to give it back.'

Which one kept her job? The good-looking one with the big tits.

Some of the 'Big Questions' that Professor Paul Davies refused to answer when posed by Phillip Adams in their TV series – and book – of the same name.

Q. How many men does it take to change a light globe?

A. One, and nine to pin the medal on his chest.

⊙

Q. Why do Aussie men give their penises names?

A. It's because they don't want 95 per cent of their decisions made by a stranger.

⊙

Q. What do you call 100 Aussie men standing in a paddock?

A. A vacant lot.

❶

Q. Why do Aussie men suffer from premature ejaculation?

A. Because they can't wait to get to the pub to tell their mates about it.

❶

Q. What do you call ten blondes standing ear to ear?

A. A wind tunnel.

①

Q. How do you give a blonde a brain transplant?

A. Blow through her ear.

①

Q. How do you make a blonde laugh on Monday morning?

A. Tell her a joke Friday night.

○

Q. How many blondes does it take to make a chocolate chip cookie?

A. Thirteen. One to mix the dough, and twelve to peel the Smarties.

○

Q. How can you tell a blonde has been using your computer?

A. There's white-out on the screen.

Q. Why are all dumb-blonde jokes one-liners?

A. So men can understand them.

THE LAST LAUGH

The Governor-General was visiting the State House for the Confused. In the main assembly hall the inmates were sitting about quietly but periodically one would stand up and shout out a number after which they would all fall about in paroxysms of mirth.

When the G-G asked what was going on, the superintendent revealed that because they had all been there so long and had heard all their respective stories many times, they had numbered them. So all an individual had to do was shout out the number of his story and they all knew what it was about.

Fascinated, the G-G said he would like to tell a story and see the reaction. The superintendent said, 'Okay, think of a number and when I introduce you, shout it out.'

Having got the attention of the audience, the superintendent introduced the G-G and announced he was going to tell a story. The G-G then shouted '69', which was greeted with a deathly silence.

Embarrassed, the official party left the hall and, when outside, the G-G asked why they hadn't laughed.

'They knew the story,' the superintendent consoled him, 'they just didn't like the way you told it!'